Adventures in Home Selling

Bert Levi

ADVENTURES IN HOME SELLING

ACKNOWLEDGMENTS

A book like this doesn't come about in a vacuum, and a number of people played a role both in the words you read and the philosophies and outlook that characterize how it was written. The list is exhaustive and there's no way for me to note everyone but I want to specifically acknowledge the tremendous help from my wife Gloria and our daughters Sophia and Sarah. I want to thank Rabbi and Mrs. Ezagui of Chabad La Jolla as well. My parents, Eddie and Rosa Levi, are (and have always been) extremely supportive. Thanks to all my employees and associates and thank you as well to Jerry, who helped me organize my thoughts.

ADVENTURES IN HOME SELLING

ABOUT BERT LEVI

Bert Levi has decades of business experience focusing on relationships people have with each other. He cares about relationships and the things important to them. His work in real estate continues that perspective, this time with a focus on the relationships people have with places. In fact, he became a real estate agent for that reason. For Bert, his family always comes first and he lives with them in La Jolla, California. If you'd like to reach Bert, you can email him at BertLevi@gmail.com or you can call him at 619-227-6201. Bert is an agent (DRE#01802687) with Lloyd Realty Group (DRE#01897519.)

INTRODUCTION

I wrote this book because of the encouragement I received after publishing my first two books, Adventures in Home Buying and Adventures in Property Investment. Those books, for the most part, focused on the ways people bought homes and other properties. The real estate business is, of course, far more than just buying and I thought exploring relationships in regards to home sales would be an interesting and exciting idea. If you read my first or second book, you already know I have always been fascinated by people and relationships. For most of my life, I have been in the jewelry industry and that has given me the privilege to play a small role in a great many relationships as I provided engagement rings, wedding bands and gifts for special occasions. I've been in the real estate business as well, and relationships are just as important there.

Just as in the jewelry business I care more about relationships and people than gold, platinum, or diamonds; I care more about relationships in real estate than anything else. I thought exploring the relationships people have with each other and places was a good idea and I'm thankful my first two books were well received.

In this book, I'll again be exploring relationships in regards to real estate but this one will focus on selling homes. Once again, I should make sure you understand this is not a typical real estate book. This book won't give you all the information you need to sell your home. I cannot stress enough that you will need to do a lot more reading if that is your goal. I wrote this book to talk about people, how home sale decisions might make them feel and might impact their lives.

There is a disclaimer at the beginning of this book but let me add to it here. Under no circumstances should you rely on anything in this book as complete information or even as information directly relevant to your situation. Real estate purchase, investment and sale are not things a story can express completely. You must get professional help in many circumstances, especially because almost every property transaction has legal or tax implications. Please keep that in mind when you read.

I express things in stories because I believe stories are a great way to share ideas and concepts. Storytelling has been a teaching tool for as long as recorded history. In fact, oral history was told through stories, and it was the only history people had before the printed press. It is my sincere hope that some of what I write will get you to think about options that might work for you, your family and your particular situation.

I hope the stories here will inspire you to ask the right questions and think about the situations that might be right for you.

THE STORIES

Table of Contents

Finding a Real Estate Agent 5

Some Stories about Selling 26

Open House Stories 48

Stories about Curb Appeal 70

For Sale by Owner 92

Tales of Owner Financing 114

Special Selling Situations 136

More Stories about Selling 158

Finding a Real Estate Agent

OLIVIA FINDS AN AGENT

Olivia never expected to sell a home before she ever bought one! In her second year of college, right after midterms, Olivia got news that a great uncle of hers had passed away and left a house to the youngest heir in college. She thought it was a strange bequest, especially because she had never met him! There were two things she knew for certain. First, she was grateful for the man she'd never met. His generosity was going to help her graduate college without any debt. The second thing she knew was that she couldn't possibly handle the sale of the home! It was located seven states away. She had a few weeks before the next semester, though, so she got a discount flight to take a look at the property. It was in a nice little neighborhood and seemed very well maintained. She knew there had to be a buyer for it but she had no idea how to go about selling it and certainly didn't have the time or money to fly back and forth! Without a lot of confidence, she searched for local real estate agents and decided to make appointments with several to see who should list the property. She settled on the agent who asked questions. It was important to her. The others talked about everything they could do. The agent she hired asked what goals she had and what she hoped would happen. There was something amazing about that kind of concern and she listed the house with him right then. A few months later, she was glad she did when offers arrived, and when the house sold and she saw all of her college expenses were covered; she was ecstatic!

Tip: A good real estate agent will ask you a great many questions. They will help you understand the sale process of course but to do that, they should first listen. Here are some thoughts.

1. Is the agent looking to list your home really interested in you? What confidence do you have the agent will look after your interests?

2. Time may be very important to you. You may want your agent to handle all of the day to day issues or you may want more involvement. If your agent doesn't ask questions, how will he or she know?

3. Remember a real estate agent is there to serve your interests. It is critical the agent actually knows what your interests are.

AMELIA AND NOAH SEEK SOME HELP

Amelia and Noah knew it was time to sell their home. They had just said goodbye to the twins, and with all of their children now in college, they had a four bedroom home just for the two of them. They almost owned the home free and clear as well. It seemed to them it was time to downsize. They could buy a more modest home that would be certain to better fit their needs and simultaneously set a good amount of money aside toward retirement. They'd still have plenty left over to help all four of their children will college expenses. To them, that seemed like a pretty good win/win situation, and they were excited about it. Noah had built three successful businesses from the ground up so it was only natural that he decided he would handle the sale himself. Six months later, the home still had not sold. It took a bit of humility for him to accept that he needed help but Amelia helped. She pointed out that he still worked fifty or sixty hours a week and couldn't devote the time to it. She worked full time, too. Ultimately, a real estate agent would be a good investment for them. He was still reluctant but they did some research and got an agent. Nick was amazed at how much it helped just to be able to focus on his normal day-to-day work without stress about selling the home. He couldn't argue with the results, either. In short order, the offers poured in and three months later, when they were settled in their new and more manageable home, both of them were grateful they had taken the step.

Tip: Although selling a home without an agent can work for some people, statistically it does not enjoy the same success when there is an agent. Here are some thoughts.

1. Keep in mind there is an investment of time and energy and even money to sell a home. That may not fit into your current situation.

2. Keep in mind a real estate agent is trained in home sales and is also the beneficiary of experience. All of that works on your behalf when you want to sell.

3. Hiring an agent does not actually remove you from decision making. You will still get to make decisions about sales and pricing. Your agent will advise you but cannot make those decisions for you.

ISLA AND HARRY FIND AN AGENT

Isla did not take the promotion immediately. She asked for a week to think it over and her employer was very happy to give her the time. The problem was the promotion meant moving halfway across the country. The problem was Harry would have to quit his job and find a new one or see if his company had possibilities in the new location. She was certainly not going to make the decision on her own. After discussion and research, though, it became clear that it was the best decision for them. That meant they had to sell their home but they could not do it without help because the promotion meant they would have to move very quickly. They had to act fast, and that is exactly what they did. Harry went online and Isla called friends and associates who might know good agents. It still took a few weeks. In fact, they signed the listing agreement in an empty house because the movers already had everything packed up! They chose an agent who understood their needs and had a reputation for trustworthiness, and it paid off. They were just settling into their new home when they got news of a great offer. Everything seemed perfect!

Tip: There are a number of ways to find an agent but the number one thing to remember is to find one who pays attention to your goals and needs.

1. Remember that real estate agents represent you. That means they should focus on your needs, not on fitting you into their goals.

2. One of the best ways to find an agent is to speak to your friends and acquaintances. Chances are many have used agents and can make recommendations.

3. Remember in addition to the agent, you should also consider the brokerage firm for which the agent works.

AN AGENT FOR EMILY AND JACK

Emily and Jack wanted to sell their home but they did not really know how to go about making it happen. Jack's parents gave them the home when they retired to Florida so they had not actually ever purchased it and had no experience with the process. They wondered how to find a real estate agent. There were signs everywhere but those signs always represented a property that was already listed. What were they to do? After trying to figure the situation out, they finally decided they had to take action, and in this case taking action meant they had to start somewhere. It did not take as much work as they thought. Simply by calling agents they found on signs advertising, they got a number of possibilities but they were still frustrated because the agents seem to treat them like "fresh meat." Finally, an agent arrived and took them through the sales process, everything they could expect. It opened their eyes to what it meant to sell a house and to what it was like to have an agent who would actually serve their interests! They signed with her and four months later, they prepared to move into their new home!

Tip: More than most services you will engage in your life, special skills are needed in real estate agents. Here are some questions to ask.

1. Can you please explain what actions you will take from the moment I sign the listing agreement?

2. What plans do you have to make my home more marketable?

3. Can you give me examples of times you sold a home like mine?

4. Tell me what services you actually provide, please. What is included in your service?

AVA AND JACOB AND SOMEBODY GOOD

Ava and Jacob decided they would find the best possible real estate agent when it came time to sell their home. They would be moving in eleven months and they wanted to sell and, if need be, simply travel while they waited for their new home to be available. That was plenty of time, they thought, for a great real estate agent. In a few weeks, though, they realized there were a lot of great real estate agents available! They met with several and they were about to hire one but wanted to keep their word with a last appointment. They ended up hiring that person! The difference for them was learning that a brokerage firm providing support to an agent could make a real difference in the ability of the agent to succeed. It seemed like a great thing to the two of them, and Ava and Jacob were looking forward to seeing how the help of support staff, experience and technology provided by the brokerage firm would help with the sale of their home. It truly helped, too! In fact, they discovered very quickly that it made a big difference because there were agents at the office who had potential buyers! They would be travelling for a number of months.

Tip: A great agent is wonderful but you should also consider the resources available to the agent from his or her brokerage firm.

1. Brokerage firms have support personnel like secretaries, accountants and, in some cases, creative departments.

2. Brokerage firms have a wealth of experience available. If your agent encounters something new, there is a lot to draw on for help.

3. Brokerage firms make sure agents are kept up to date with new laws and policies.

SOMEONE TO HELP LILY AND CHARLIE

If there was one thing that became apparent to Lilly and Charlie very quickly, it was that they couldn't do it without help. They could put up a sign that the home was for sale and they could even put it on a website or two but that did not seem like it would be enough. In fact, after two months without a single inquiry at all, they knew they would have to find someone who could lead them to success. So, they asked some friends and some associates if they knew any agents. They got a few choices and from there, they did some research. They checked online reviews and they checked the websites of each agent. They met with several and took notes. They narrowed down their list and asked for referrals. From there, they asked for some prior clients and got an even better picture of the two or three agents they'd narrowed down. When it was all said and done, they were confident they chose the right agent, and they were excited to know that they could rest easy knowing the agent was working on selling their home for them, working hard on their behalf.

Tip: Don't neglect the research! Real estate agents are like any other professionals. There are great agents and agents who are not so great. Here are some thoughts.

1. The very best place to start is with the agent's website. What does it tell you about their professionalism and their freeness with information to help you?

2. Online reviews can be helpful but keep in mind that in most cases, people who leave reviews are either very happy or very unhappy. It only gives you a picture of the extremes of an agent's history.

3. Perhaps the best way to learn about an agent's practice is to ask for prior clients. Ask specifically if they can include a client who is not satisfied.

MIA AND FREDDIE LIST THEIR HOME

Mia's hand trembled as she signed the agreement with the real estate agent. Freddie's hand was a little bit steadier but she knew it was just as difficult for him. This was a very big decision, selling their home. Once the decision was made, choosing somebody to help was also a very big decision. They had worked for seven years to be able to afford the home they would sell and they had lived there for almost a decade. They needed someone who would take that seriously and that meant knowing what the agent would do to help them. They met with a number of agents but they went with the agent who was willing to give them specific plans for the marketing of the house. They were very impressed with her, especially since most of the other agents spoke only in generalities. They were thankful for the specifics but it still felt a little nerve wracking to make the final decision. They knew it was the right thing, though, and their instincts were correct. In only a few months, the house was in escrow because the agent did exactly what she said she would do!

Tip: You have the right to find out what an agent is doing to market your home and to ensure they are representing your interests. Here are some ideas for you.

1. Ask the agent what specific steps they will take to market your home. If they are unwilling to give you specifics, you may want to pass.

2. Ask the agent deeper questions, too. If they say they will put up signs, ask how many. If they say they will call potential clients, ask how many. If they say they will put the home on websites, find out which ones.

3. Above all else, remember that your agent works for you. That means you deserve a clear understanding of what will happen.

GRACE AND ALFIE WANT TO SELL

It had taken a long time for Grace and Alfie to decide to sell their home. They were attached to it even though they knew they needed to move to a larger home. They had two kids now and with two dogs as well, they had to change tack. In addition, it seemed like maybe Grace's aunt would need some care and they thought having a room available if she needed to move in was a good idea. A good friend had just sold a home so they had a great recommendation for a real estate agent and they were glad they found him! Almost immediately, offers started coming but there were things they did not understand like owner carrybacks, financing contingencies and backup offers. Fortunately, the agent understood all of those things and, more importantly, knew how to explain those things to Grace and Alfie. That was really the key. They weren't just making decisions based on their agent's recommendations but based on knowledge he imparted to them. It made the whole process easier, which made the celebration when it sold a whole lot more fun.

Tip: You can negotiate just about any deal in real estate. That gives you a great deal of flexibility but it also explains why a real estate agent can be such a tremendous help. Keep these things in mind.

1. Although there are infinite ways to structure a real estate deal, the legal and tax implications can be hard to understand. An agent can help.

2. You will likely never have heard of some of the things buyers might suggest. It is highly likely your agent has experience with them.

3. Agents can help you navigate laws that are complicated even when a sale is simple. When a sale is complicated, agents are critical!

SOPHIA AND GEORGE NEED A HAND

Sophia and George did not know what to do. Sometimes it felt like their home would never sell. They were very happy when their listing agreement with a real estate agent expired. They decided they not only had to get a new agent but they had to understand what the agent would do. They certainly did not want an agent who did not return their calls in a timely fashion like the last one! So, when they contacted real estate agents the second time, they were very clear. They wanted to know what would be done. They wanted a plan and they wanted to be convinced that the plan would work. Sophia thought if a real estate agent could not sell them on the plan, there was no way the agent would be able to sell the house. That made sense to George and that was their strategy. When they found an agent they were confident in, they crossed their fingers and waited. They discovered the difference pretty quickly. After only a month, inquiries started coming in. Within another month, the house was in escrow. They found an agent with a plan and stuck with it!

Tip: Selling a home without help can be a real challenge. When you realize you need help from a real estate agent, there are some thoughts you should keep in mind.

1. There are a great many real estate agents out there and a lot of information online about what makes an agent great. Don't feel trapped with an agent who doesn't appeal to you.

2. Make sure to ask your agent what specific actions they will take to sell your home. Make sure you get specifics and not just general statements.

3. Your agent should have a plan. If they cannot explain the plan to you, how confident can you be about them explaining the value of your property to a buyer?

ISABELLA AND FREDDIE SIGN ON THE DOTTED LINE

It took a very long time for Isabella and Freddie to choose a real estate agent to help them sell their home. It just seemed like every one of them they encountered cared more about getting a signature than actually helping them understand the services they would receive. They felt like they were at their wits end but a friend of Isabella's at the office told her about a great agent who had helped her sell. They figured they would give that agent a try. When they met with her, they could see right away there was a big difference in the way she did business. She started out asking questions, making sure she understood what they wanted to happen. Even more than that, she took an interest in their life like she expected to be a part of it long after the home sold. That made sense after closing, though, because they knew they would send anyone who ever asked to their agent and the next time they had any real estate need at all, they knew they would be calling her!

Tip: When you sign on with a real estate agent, you should keep in mind they ought to not only think about your current transaction but your relationship as a whole.

1. Agents who succeed think past a single transaction. They want to make sure you are very happy because statistically, you are likely to need real estate services again.

2. An agent who values you will realize that you not only represent the individual sale but also a great many people you might influence with a recommendation.

3. Most importantly, an agent should have your best interests in mind because that is what you pay them for!

Some Stories about Selling

ARTHUR AND IVY SELL THEIR HOME

Arthur and Ivy were about as excited as they could be. They knew the new job was going to be wonderful and they were excited because it took them back to their hometown! Of course, that meant they had to sell their home but they were confident that would not be a problem. Five months later, they were not quite as confident. They had two seller back out and it looked like their current seller was not going to be able to close. They had been so excited in the beginning but now, they had to admit they really just wanted the situation to be over. It might not have been the smartest thing but that was how they felt. Already, Arthur had to fly back to his home town and only return on weekends. When would it end! Their agent finally had a long conversation. He was confident the bank would fund the current buyer if they just dropped the price a little bit. They were not happy about that but the agent explained they had already lost that much just paying their current mortgage longer than they expected. That did the trick. They made the change and two weeks later the sale closed. All the excitement came back and they were able to move right on to their own happily ever after.

Tip: When you want to sell your home, one of the most important things you can do is manage your expectations. Keep a few things in mind.

1. Remember that homes represent a very large purchase. For the most part, people do not make those decisions quickly.

2. Remember that there are a lot of moving parts in a sale. The key is really remaining patient.

3. Sometimes, the market just will not allow you to get the price you would like to get.

RUBY AND THOMAS AND THE SALE

Ruby and Thomas felt frustrated because it seemed like there was no movement in the sale of their home. They really wanted to see things move forward but it just was not happening. This was despite the fact that their agent had arranged a number of successful open house events. Finally, they got together with their agent to brainstorm ways to deal with the situation. The first thing they had to acknowledge was that their neighborhood wasn't really family friendly. There were not parks and the elementary schools were pretty far away. That meant they needed to seek out older professionals. They would be able to pay more but were often more price conscious so they decided to reduce the price by a few thousand dollars. Finally, they moved some items into storage to give the home a less cluttered appearance. Ruby and Thomas hoped the change in strategy would work, and it did! They got three offers within two weeks. It seemed like things were finally moving forward the way they should. Everything looked better now.

Tip: Agents with experience will know when it is time to change strategy. If your home generates no interest at all, there are a few things you will want to think about.

1. Oftentimes, a homeowner will need to make a decision about price. When the market does not support the price desired, a change may be needed.

2. Sometimes, a neighborhood is not attractive to some buyers. Marketing incorrectly is ineffective.

3. The best strategy at all times is to educate yourself and then rely on the advice from your agent that you understand.

POPPY AND MASON SELL THEIR HOME

Sometimes, it only takes a tiny change to make a home very marketable. In the case of Poppy and Mason, all it took was taking a bed out of a small room and replacing it with a desk! Their four-bedroom home just did not seem to generate interest once someone saw it. When they positioned one room as an office, though, the offers started pouring in! Something that seemed like a small bedroom suddenly seemed like a large office, and that not only appealed to people who wanted an office at home but also to people who thought they could use the office as a bedroom instead. It was really amazing, and Mason and Poppy knew they had an experienced real estate agent to thank for the change. It did not take long before they had the home in escrow and when the home sold, they were absolutely thrilled. Now, they could move on to the next stage of their life and they knew they had opportunities that seemed absolutely endless. Who would have thought putting a desk where a bed used to be would do that?

Tip: Oftentimes, even the very smallest change can make a very significant difference in your home sale. The key is listening to your agent's advice and carefully considering it.

1. Even if you have sold three or four personal residences, your agent will have experienced far more sales situations than you have.

2. Small changes seem unimportant sometimes. They often make a very big difference.

3. Think of times you bought something because of how possibilities were revealed to you. Can you do that with your house?

FINLEY HAS GREAT NEWS FOR CHARLOTTE

Charlotte and Finley were a bit worried. Their home had been on the market for quite some time and things were not moving forward. Oddly, a potential buyer had visited the home several times but it seemed like he was just not willing to make an offer. Finley asked the agent to find out why. The answer was surprising. The buyer was going to use all of his available cash for the down payment on the home. He loved the home. However, he would not be able to furnish it, and that was the only hold up. He did not want his kids sleeping on the floor! The agent asked how committed Charlotte and Finley were to their furniture. He said if they offered to include it in the purchase for a few thousand dollars more, the bank loan would cover it and the buyer could move forward. They thought they might as well give it a shot because they had planned to replace their furniture over the next year anyway. That did the trick, and it was a real win-win. The buyer and seller both ended up with the furniture they needed!

Tip: Sometimes, when it seems like you are at an impasse with a buyer there simply needs to be a little more consideration to the real motives at play. Here are some thoughts.

1. Oftentimes, potential buyers believe the only negotiable point is price, and so they do not communicate what they need.

2. When you seek for win-win solutions to your transaction, you are likely to be successful.

3. Do not be afraid to give your agent direction. It is perfectly appropriate in some circumstances to say, "Find out why."

JESSICA AND TEDDY AND A HOUSE ON THE MOUNTAIN

Jessica and Teddy had not planned on moving. However, they both worked at home and were both very successful so they were not really tied down to any particular location. On a camping trip, they drove by a home for sale in a little mountain town and, on a lark, called the agent. When they toured the home on their way back from camping, Jessica fell in love with it. Teddy loved it to but he pointed out the only way they would be able to buy it would be to sell their other home. They told the real estate agent who showed them the mountain home that they wanted the home but had to sell the other home. They would make an offer now but it could take a few months to sell the other home. Fortunately, the buyer was willing to give them an option to buy. They paid a fee and they would be able to try to buy the home if any offers that matched theirs came in before their home sold. They listed it with the same agent, so he was double motivated! It all worked out. Their first home sold and they got their dream home. Life was beautiful, Teddy thought, just like Jessica!

Tip: While making an offer for a new home contingent on the sale of an old home, there are no guarantees the home will sell in time. Keep some things in mind.

1. As long as you communicate effectively, most buyers will work with you on timing with the close.

2. NEVER try to hide circumstances that might impact your ability to close. Always be up front.

3. Your agent can help you make an attractive offer even with a sale contingency.

WILLIAM'S BEAUTIFUL DAISY

William loved Daisy. He loved her more than he could even imagine and he wanted to do something very special for her. She had always wanted a home with a very large playroom for the kids. On her birthday, William wanted to present her with four possibilities and to start the process of choosing one. He met with an agent and the agent helped him sort out the choices. The agent also helped him understand what would need to happen to sell the home where they lived. It was a lot of work and a struggle to get it all ready for her birthday but they managed, and boy was Daisy happy! She stared in wonder at her husband as they looked at the homes. She thought about a big Christmas tree loaded with toys for the playroom, and just a few months later, that was exactly what she got! Daisy thought things could not get any better. As for William, he already knew there was nothing better than the sight of Daisy's beautiful smile. He knew he would be seeing more of it in their brand-new beautiful home.

Tip: There might be nothing quite as exciting as the feeling of buying or selling a home. It really is great news, and here are a few ideas about how you might celebrate.

1. Have the family work together on deciding decorating choices. This gives everyone a sense of ownership.

2. Throw a housewarming party! This is a way to show off your new home and give everyone a chance to enjoy your new place.

3. Make plans for the backyard or a special room. This is sure to excite all the members of the family.

SOPHIE AND JAMES AND THEIR HOME SELLING EXPERIENCE

Sophie and James were ready to throw up their hands. They got several offers but almost all of them were either confusing or simply well below the price they needed to get. They met with their agent because they did not know how much more they could handle! He took a lot of time to go over the offers in detail so they would really understand them. Then, he said he only saw two options available to end the frustration. Either they needed to drop the price a little or they needed to be willing to carry back a portion of the purchase price as an owner-financed note. Of course, if neither of those was acceptable to them, he was happy to keep things exactly the same and just get through the frustration until they got an offer they were happy with. The two talked it over and decided they would be willing to carry back a portion of the price. Once that was determined, their home opened escrow. They were amazed at how smoothly everything went! It was not what they expected but it all worked out wonderfully.

Tip: Selling a home can be a wonderful experience or a terrible experience. Here are some thoughts to help you make it wonderful.

1. You may need to consider your pricing. That might be the number one issue involved in delays in a sale.

2. Remember that you should always be in control of the sale. It is fine to expect your agent to keep you appraised with everything that happens as it happens.

3. Do not allow frustration with the process to keep you from making the right decisions. Frustration can cause you to make poor decisions just to finish things.

HENRY AND FREYA NEED A LARGER HOME

Although they loved their little starter home, the baby was not really a baby anymore! He was almost ready to start school and now Henry and Freya were expecting another baby. They needed a home a little bigger, hopefully with a big backyard that their kids could enjoy. It was hard for them, though. Henry loved the landscaping he had done. He spent many Saturdays with plants and decorations. He loved it! As for Freya, she thought about all the nights they had enjoyed on the back porch and all the time she had put into her garden, shooing Henry away so he would not try to change things. She thought about how the kids loved the house. It was hard to let go and hard to believe the new home would feel like home. When the home sold and they moved into their new home, though, their agent seemed to know just what they had to hear. She told them she was looking forward to getting some vegetables with the garden's first harvest and she expected to see an incredible front yard in a few months. It brought a smile to Freya's face. The new house was not a home yet. But it would be!

Tip: Sometimes you sell a wonderful home that just no longer meets your needs. Here are some ideas to help you make your new house a home as well.

1. Make a list of decorating choices and changes you would like right away.

2. Get the whole family involved in projects like landscaping the backyard or decorating common areas.

3. Do not live out of boxes for very long at all! Get those pictures on the wall. Get things normal as soon as you can.

ALICE AND LOGAN GO FOR IT!

Alice and Logan could not believe the way the market for real estate had grown. They had, for some time, planned to move back to their hometown sometime in the future. Now, with their home so valuable and so much equity involved, they thought it might make sense to make the move a few years ahead of schedule. They were pretty sure they could buy a home free and clear in their small home town just with the appreciation of the home they owned now! The problem was that the decision seemed so enormous. It almost paralyzed them. They wanted to do it but on the other hand they did not know if it was a good idea or a bad idea. Mostly, they were just worried about making the wrong decision. What pushed them over the edge was actually a knock at the door on a Saturday afternoon. A smiling real estate agent introduced herself and said she sold a number of homes in the neighborhood. She wanted to let them have her card just in case they had needs in the future. She was surprised to discover they had needs right then! The decision was made.

Tip: Sometimes, we just need a little push to get moving in the right direction. If you are on the fence, here are some ideas about how to make a difficult decision.

1. Although a home's value can be a big factor, think about how your current location impacts your life.

2. Set a date to make the decision. That decision is either yes, no or wait for a period of time before revisiting it.

3. Remember that some agents will try to pressure you to make a listing or a sale. It is important you express your needs and stick to your guns.

ISABELLE LEAVES HER STARTER HOME

How was she supposed to leave the home she loved? It was such a difficult decision for her but she knew it was the right thing to do. She had two kids and they were both in school now. Her husband's overseas deployment was almost over, and that meant he'd be home full time, stationed stateside for three years. Whether or not he reenlisted, the home was too small now. She had built a pretty successful business, too, and an office would mean she would not have to do the work at the kitchen table! She had an Internet call with her husband and he told her he trusted her to handle everything. He would sign whatever he needed to sign. She felt wonderful that he trusted her and she got started but she still felt wistful about missing the home she loved. She had to do it, though. As far as she was concerned, it was an absolute necessity. So, she called her best friend, who had just sold her home, and her friend introduced her to the agent who handled it. The week after her husband returned from overseas, they signed the closing documents on their new home. She knew she would always miss her first home but she also knew the new house would be a perfect home soon enough!

Tip: Moving to a larger home or a nicer neighborhood is a great milestone in a person's life, and one of the best things you can do to celebrate that is to make your new home something really, really special. Here are some quick thoughts.

1. If you miss the coziness of your first home, remember you can decorate cozy nooks in your new home! Coziness has a lot to do with outlook more than size.

2. Do not think that you are boxed in! You can make decisions about your home and your decorations. Make the place yours!

3. Get the whole family involved! Make sure everyone, youngest to oldest, is able to be heard.

Open House Stories

ADAM AND ARIA OPEN UP THEIR HOME

In preparation for their open house, Adam and Aria had a list of things to do. Their agent suggested they might want to take some of their furniture and put it in storage for a while. They had eclectic tastes, and though a cluttered look really worked for them, it made the home seem smaller. So, they took down some of the knick knacks and put a few pieces of furniture in storage. When they were done, they had to admit the house looked a lot bigger. They never would have believed such a small trick would have such a big impact. They had their carpets cleaned as well. It did not cost very much at all but it, too, seemed to open things up. Last and not least, their backyard was overgrown because they almost never went out there. So, they got that addressed as well. When they were finished, they had to admit the whole place looked a lot more attractive and looked a lot larger as well. That made them feel confident the place would sell quickly!

Tip: When you want a successful open house, you want to do the things that will make your home appeal to potential buyers. Here are some things to consider.

1. Did you know model homes have furniture smaller than what is sold at furniture stores? Use the same principle. Less is more.

2. Keeping things neat and tidy is critical for the same reason. Toys on the floor, for example, make a room seem smaller.

3. Ask your agent which rooms need to be opened up a little bit.

ALBIE AND ELLIE AND THE OPEN HOUSE

Albie and Ellie loved entertaining, so the idea of having an open house was exciting for them. They had a great many parties and so they just thought of the open house the same way. Their agent told them he really liked their enthusiasm but he gave them some advice. Though their agent told them not to arrange the furniture the way they might for a party, Albie brought out the barbecue and cooked all day. In the end, it worked out because offers came in from people who, just like Albie and Ellie, loved to entertain. It also meant people spent more time in the backyard of the house and the backyard was probably the best feature the house had. They thought it was a really wonderful success, and their agent agreed. They looked over the multiple offers and decided on which one they would accept. Their agent had warned them that the open house might not result in an offer so they were very happy and pleasantly surprised. They were even happier when the house closed and they were able to move on to their new home!

Tip: One great thing about an open house is that it gives the potential buyers to see how the home might feel with a group of people inside. Keep this in mind.

1. Although you might arrange chairs to ensure interaction during a party, people will want to see the house as it might look day to day if they bought it.

2. Make sure you speak with your agent about the best strategies with an open house. You will want to make decisions together using the agent's experience.

3. Do not forget refreshments even if your agent says they will take care of it. You do not have to go overboard but you will be glad to have some available!

ALEXANDER AND SOFIA WELCOME GUESTS

Alexander and Sofia tended to stay at home by themselves for quiet evenings. Really, their social lives were limited to very few friends they felt close to and saw infrequently. So, the idea of an open house was a little bit scary for them. They could not think of a time when their home had more than five adults inside at once! They also had four kids and they loved spending time with them more than anything else. The idea of an open house was scary but their agent was very helpful. She told them they would definitely want to help their children enjoy themselves because if they were forced to sit quietly for hours, that might be torture! Sofia laughed because it was absolutely true. In the end, she called her brother and the kids ended up spending the day with their uncle. They arrived near the end of the open house, happy and excited. They were able to have a lot of fun and they did not have to just wait around or take up their parents' attention when they were busy with the sale.

Tip: Do not forget that you may have dozens of guests in your home for the open house. Make sure you have arranged for activities for your kids!

1. Your children enjoying themselves in the backyard with the pets could actually be a great selling point.

2. You may consider planning an outing for them so they are not bored and expected to be on their best behavior all day long.

3. Generally, kids will want to help. You will want to keep an eye on things to avoid mishaps.

CARTER AND ERIN HOLD THE EVENT

Since they owned an event planning business, Carter and Erin were sure they knew everything that needed to happen for their open house. In fact, they opened a project management spreadsheet and got right to work. When they presented the ideas to their agent, they learned that they were probably overcomplicating things. The most important thing they could do would be to make the home as appealing as they could. In fact, things that would make an event like a wedding or a business conference go very well could make an open house a failure! So, they backed away and decided they would just respond to the agent's direction. They were very happy they did as well. The open house went very well, and over the next week, they received several offers. It was a real joy to spend time trying to decide which offer to take instead of just waiting around to just get one. They knew the home would sell soon, and they were so happy they did not try to take over the open house.

Tip: The most important thing about an open house is the impression your home will give to the buyers. Work with your agent to determine what that impression should be.

1. Sometimes, a thorough cleaning is in order. The home may not need a lot of housework but it could be some extra shine on the furniture is a great idea.

2. Your agent may suggest some rugs or runners over areas of tile that are likely to get a lot of traffic.

3. Getting rid of clutter is probably the number one thing you can do to make your home more attractive during an open house.

DANIEL AND LOLA MEET THEIR POTENTIAL BUYERS

Daniel and Lola were excited about their open house and the only real question left was what they would do about Chief and Sunny, their two beautiful German shepherds. They were part of the family and even though they were very well-behaved dogs, they knew sometimes people were afraid just because Chief and Sunny were high energy. Their agent suggested keeping their pets somewhere else during the open house might be a good idea. The fact that they could not make an immediate decision goes to show just how much they loved the dog. In the end, the shepherds ended up with Lola's father, and he took them two days ahead of time. That gave Daniel and Lola plenty of time to make sure the backyard was clean and there were not any pet odors in the house. The moment the open house was over, they rushed to Lola's dad's place to get their babies. Chief and Sunny were happy and excited and by the time they got home, Daniel and Lola were excited, too. The open house resulted in some offers!

Tip: Do not forget to think about your pets on the day of your open house. You may want to board them somewhere. You definitely want to make sure of a few things.

1. If you are going to keep your pet at the home for the open house, make sure it is groomed and happy.

2. If your pet has any trouble with people, safety first! Board your pet to keep everyone safe.

3. Be very concerned about potential pet odors during the open house. Ask your agent to check because you may be so familiar with it you do not actually smell it anymore.

DAVID AND LILLY THROW AN IMPORTANT PARTY

David and Lilly threw a lot of parties but they had never thrown a party with a purpose other than celebration or just fun. Now, though, they had an open house upcoming. Their agent said they should not worry about entertaining the people who attended. The most important thing they could do would be to instead just make sure the home was as presentable as it could possibly be. They were a bit obsessive about organization and cleanliness so there was not much work to do in that department. However, they had some art that was geared toward adults, and the agent recommended they put those pieces away in case there were children who arrived with their parents. In addition, she suggested David and Lilly might want to put some throw pillows out and perhaps a fruit bowl or something along those lines to make the house seem a bit more homey. They followed the advice and even though the décor an ambiance did not really fit their personality, they could not argue with the results because the open house led to three offers!

Tip: An open house can be a wonderful asset or a terrible liability. Here are some thoughts to help you make yours something positive.

1. This seems obvious but make sure the house is clean! Although it does not necessarily make sense, people will assume a house that is not clean has problems with it.

2. Make sure you do not leave any clutter around. Clutter makes the rooms seem smaller.

3. Do your best to stay out of your agent's way during the open house. It is the agent's job to answer questions.

DYLAN AND THEA GET EVERYTHING READY

Dylan put the last box in the back of his truck and walked back into the house. He had to admit. His agent was right. The house looked a whole lot better and all it took was packing some of the things away a little bit ahead of schedule. When people arrived for the open house, they would see a roomier version of the place than Dylan usually saw. He and Thea were collectors. They had hundreds of figurines, dozens of sculptures, thousands of vinyl records and a great deal more. Though they were all neat and well-organized, they certainly filled up the house. In fact, one of the things they loved about the new house was a very large great room they would make the place where they could display their collections. Now that most of that was packed away, their home looked far more attractive. Dylan was happy he had payed attention to the real estate agent and Thea could not be happier with the decision because the open house was a roaring success!

Tip: When you have your open house, make sure you follow your agent's instructions to present your house in the best possible way for buyers.

1. There are some easy ways to make the most of your home's size and that can include packing some things away or just rearranging furniture.

2. Sometimes, a little bit of decoration can go a long way as well. Simply putting a vase of flowers out can really brighten up a room.

3. Think about the impression a potential buyer will get the moment they step into the house. This is a critical thing!

EDWARD AND IMOGEN AND THE OPEN HOUSE

It almost reminded Imogen of when she was a little girl and company was going to come over. Her mother would scrub the whole house and all the kids were recruited to help. Now, as she cleaned and got ready for the weekend open house that might result in some offers for their home, Imogen smiled at the memories of her mom and her family. She would have to make sure they all got a chance to visit her new home just as soon as possible! The new home was going to be perfect, and they would be moving in just a week. Of course, they did not want to have to maintain two mortgages so they were very eager to sell the current home, and that meant making sure the place looked its best. Edward was mowing the backyard right now, and the twins were helping, too. They were making sure the playroom and the bedroom were completely clutter free. There were beautiful memories and it was fantastic to know there would be many, many more beautiful memories to come in their new home!

Tip: You will want to make sure your home is clean and fresh on the day of your open house. Here are some areas to pay special attention.

1. The bathrooms are very important so make sure they are presentable in the best possible light. Potpourri or deodorizer for a fresh scent is critical here.

2. The kitchen should be sparkly clean and free of clutter. A bowl of fruit might be a nice touch.

3. Pay attention to often neglected areas of the home like laundry areas and closets!

ELIJAH AND ELIZA WELCOME A CROWD

Elijah and Eliza went out a great deal. In fact, when they had gotten together with friends or family, they almost always went to a restaurant or to somebody else's house. So, they told their agent they were a little bit nervous about the open house. They just did not know how to prepare for people in their home! The agent told them not to worry. He would handle almost all of the interactions. All they needed to do was to make sure their home looked open and lovely. So, they got to work. First, they made sure none of the light bulbs were out, and they bought some extra to have on hand in case any went out during the weekend. Second, they made sure to clear the home of any clutter but not to make it seem like some kind of hotel lobby! They put some decorative baskets on the end tables and set the table with their best China. They were happy with how the home looked, and their agent was happy, too. They discovered the potential buyers were also happy because they got a number of offers!

Tip: You want to present your house in the best possible light during your open house so here are a couple of things you will want to consider.

1. Make sure there are not any dark areas in the home. You will want to make sure all the lights work.

2. You can be uncluttered without being severe. A nice decorative basket with pine cones or spheres makes a difference.

3. Do not forget that people coming are trying to decide if they would like to live there. Make sure it looks like a place where someone would want to live.

FRANKIE AND BELLA FEEL WONDERFUL

The two of them really wanted to sell their house but they did not have any experience like that at all. Bella ran a pneumatic supply company and she was pretty sure selling valves and tubing was nothing like selling a home. As for Frankie, he owned a restaurant. He could sell a steak but how in the world was he supposed to sell a whole house? Fortunately, they did not need that experience. They had an agent who was happy to give them all the direction they needed. First and foremost, she gave Frankie and Bella ideas for preparing for the open house. It involved rearranging furniture and buying a carpet runner. It also involved changing the welcome mat and some door decorations in the front. Finally, cleaning the garage was necessary because nobody would be able to see inside of it. When they were done, they felt great. When the open house came, they felt really great. When the offers started arriving, they felt absolutely wonderful!

Tip: Your agent has more experience than you do with what makes an open house work. Here are some questions to ask.

1. Should the furniture be rearranged in order to show the room in the best possible light?

2. Is there any area of the house that would benefit from a small purchase like a runner or a vase of flowers?

3. Is there anything I should do in order to prepare the front yard?

Stories about Curb Appeal

OLLIE AND WILLOW MAKE THEIR HOME A LITTLE MORE BEAUTIFUL

Ollie and Willow were beginning to feel a bit worried. Their home had been on the market a while now and they did not have any offers. They intended to call their real estate agent but she showed up first and together they walked through the house. She made some very small suggestions. First, she suggested the living room seemed a little full and if they were take the loveseat out and leave just the recliner and the sofa it would likely seem bigger. She suggested they open all of the drapes before an appointment so light would stream in and the house would open up. Finally, she said getting the lawn in order would also help. With their marching orders in place, Ollie and Willow got to work. Really, there was not all that much work involved and they were very happy with the results. The yardwork did the best for them. They thought their cute house was suddenly welcoming and inviting. They were sure they would find success now!

Tip: Curb appeal is really about first impressions. Little things can often go a very long way. Here are a few ideas you might be able to use.

1. Make sure your yard is cleaned up. Mow the grass, if necessary, and make sure there are not things like bicycles or toys in the front yard.

2. Think about details. Does your address on the curb need to be repainted?

3. Are there oil stains on the driveway?

THE FIRST THING EVELYN SEES

When Evelyn hired her real estate agent, she was immediately struck by the skill of the person she hired. Her agent took her to the street and said to imagine she had never seen her house before. She was to look at her home for the very first time and think about what she saw. Evelyn closed her eyes and when she opened them, the first thing she realized was that the car needed to be washed and the lawn needed mowing. She also thought the furniture on the front porch seemed a bit old and ragged. She shared those thoughts with her agent, and he told her that was the first impression any potential buyer would have as well. With that in mind, Evelyn got to work. Before long, her yard was impeccable and with the furniture gone, her porch seemed a great deal more inviting. She added some potted plants to the porch and when she was done, she felt like her home was transformed. She was surprised at how wonderfully it worked out and excited when the offers started pouring in.

Tip: The interior of your home might be perfectly wonderful but the exterior is the very first thing your potential buyers will see. That means you want to make the impression as good as it can be!

1. Do not forget that a car covered with mud will impact the perception of the home if the car is in the driveway!

2. Sometimes, comfortable porch or lawn furniture works for you but distracts from curb appeal.

3. Make sure you try to see your home as potential buyers might. This will give you a list of tasks.

JACKSON AND SCARLETT WORK ON CURB APPEAL

Jackson and Scarlett needed to sell their home. There was no choice about it! They were relocating and every mortgage payment on the old house would dip into their savings. They hired an agent and the agent told them the interior of their home was perfect but the exterior needed work. They had started a landscaping project a few years back but never finished it. The agent said it would scare off some buyers and would give other buyers an excuse to offer less. So, they spent the next two weekends getting the work done, and when they were finished they knew the situation looked a whole lot better. The home did not seem incomplete anymore, and the look from the street was actually quite lovely. They felt a renewed surge of confidence. The way their home looked now, they were certain they would get a lot of interest. They were right. People loved the attractive outside of the home and once they got inside, they loved the interior. Before long, they got an offer and then two more after that!

Tip: Sometimes, the key to curb appeal is not all that complicated at all but is nonetheless something you might not think about at first.

1. Think about what lawn decorations you have like garden gnomes or other sculptures. Are they still bright and lovely?

2. Do you need to do some yardwork? A neglected front yard often brings the impression of a neglected house.

3. Make sure you do not have any yard projects in progress! Finish them up.

FLORENCE AND BOBBY FIND OUT IT IS SIMPLE

Florence and Bobby really wanted to sell their home because they had a great deal of equity. All of the kids were in college and they were moving to a smaller home. They wanted to use their equity in the old home to make sure all three of their kids had a substantial gift from them when they graduated. With the kids, gone, though, they had neglected the yardwork. Their real estate agent told them they would need to get the yard impeccable to offer the best possible impression for potential buyers. It was all about curb appeal, the agent said, and they would need to make that a priority. So, they got right to work. They mowed. They weeded. They swept. They did everything they could and they were happy when it was done. Florence got a few lawn decorations and a nice welcome mat. Bobby replaced the mailbox and repainted the address on the curb. When they were all done, the agent told them the house looked wonderful. Now she could get to work and get their home sold.

Tip: It can often be so simple to make your home's curb appeal a lot more attractive that we tend to overcomplicate it. Here are some thoughts.

1. It seems simple but make sure your mailbox, if you have one, is freshly painted and upright.

2. Keeping your lawn maintained can make a dramatic difference in the success of a sale.

3. Go to the street in front of your home and take a look. Would you buy what you see?

ALEX AND LAYLA MAKE IT PRETTY

Alex and Layla were both professionals and that meant, for the most part, they really only spent time at home in the evenings. That meant they really rarely saw their front yard in the daytime. When they met with their real estate agent on a Saturday morning, the agent told them to take a good look at the front of the house. As he pointed things out, they realized the house did not look very good at all. They had neglected the landscape and there were cracked and broken boards in the fence. It really was not a great deal of work but it made everything seem very run down. They got right to work, and after a week or two, they invited the agent back. This time, the agent was very happy with what he saw. The place had plenty of curb appeal now, and he was sure nothing in the home's appearance would inhibit a sale. It was a great feeling, and they were excited to do whatever they needed to do to make the sale happen.

Tip: Although beauty is definitely in the eye of the beholder, there are some universal truths about how to increase curb appeal that you should keep in mind.

1. Something that seems out of place can make a bad impression. Make sure you do not have toys, bikes or tools in the front yard.

2. Simple lawn care is very important. You do not need elaborate landscaping but the lawn should not be overgrown.

3. If there is any need for repair on the fence, you need to make that a priority.

MATILDA AND ZACHARY DO THE YARDWORK

The lawn was overgrown. Around the trees, there were a great many weeds. Weeds had grown so much in the shrubbery that they were barely visible. Matilda and Zachary could not argue with their agent when she said the yardwork had to be done. Since they usually entered from the garage, they had not needed to walk the path from the driveway to the front door. Once they did, they could tell things had gotten out of hand. So, they pulled out the yard tools, the edger and the mower and they got to work. It was not that difficult, really. In fact, it did not take much time at all before they were laughing and enjoying each other as they made the yard beautiful again. It was wonderful. It was absolutely wonderful, and the two of them felt like it was a date. When they were finished, they had to admit the house looked a whole lot better from the curb. They had a lot of confidence, and that confidence was well placed. Before they knew it, there were offers coming in!

Tip: Simply taking care of your yard before a potential buyer sees it can go a long way to helping you gain interest in your home. Here are some things to consider.

1. Cleaning up weeds around shrubs, flowerbeds and trees goes a long way to improving the look of your yard.

2. Make sure the lawn is neatly mowed. An overgrown lawn makes a bad impression and can drive potential buyers away.

3. Keep in mind that a first impression can influence the entire outlook a potential buyer might have.

JAYDEN AND ROSIE RAKE UP SOME APPEAL

One of the best-selling points about Jayden and Rosie's home was the yard. There were five lovely oak trees that provided wonderful shade and also looked simply beautiful. There were squirrels and birds, too, and it made the home completely lovely. However, they listed their home in the autumn, and that meant leaves all over the yard! The messy appearance could diminish the loveliness. They raked every day to keep on top of it, and they had to admit it had a pretty dramatic impact on the curb appeal. What attracted them about the trees was highlighted and they still got the lovely red, orange and yellow colors on the leaves. In fact, the front yard had never seemed better. Their agent was very pleased and they loved that the very first thing any potential buyer said was that the front yard was beautiful. They knew curb appeal was not the only thing but they also knew it was a real advantage for them. When offers started coming in, they knew the raking was worth it!

Tip: Everyone is different and some people like an immaculately groomed yard while others like things a bit more natural. When you sell, though, you want your yard well maintained. Here are some thoughts.

1. Remember that your agent can tell you what people in your area prefer.

2. In general, you want a lawn clear of leaves and debris because it tends to look messy.

3. People tend to notice flaws first and advantages second. Keep that in mind when you think about curb appeal.

HARVEY AND ESME CLEAN THINGS UP

It seemed like fixing the shutters in the front window had been on Harvey's list since they moved in. Of course, there was also the problem with the brass address plaque right next to the doorway. Somehow, those little issues became almost invisible as the months and years went by. Now that they were selling the house, though, it was time for action. They might not have even noticed if their real estate agent had not suggested to them they needed to increase their curb appeal. Suddenly, the little problems became bit priorities! Harvey felt foolish as he got things done. It really was not all that much work at all. Esme was happy as she replaced a shutter. It did not take much effort at all but it the home looked so much better. When they were finished with everything, they were amazed. It was almost like they were looking at an entirely different house. They were happy and so was their real estate agent. The curb appeal was right where it needed to be and they had a lot of confidence about capturing buyers' interest.

Tip: Although yards often have toys, bicycles and other things in plain view, when it comes time to sell, you really want to keep your front yard and the front of your home uncluttered.

1. Make those minor repairs that nonetheless make your home seem messy or even dilapidated.

2. Try to look at the front yard with fresh eyes. Often, small problems can become invisible to a resident.

3. It is usually a very good idea to have your agent or a trusted friend provide a different set of eyes for you.

ALBERT AND EVA AND SOME MINOR REPAIRS

Albert and Eva loved their little home but it made a lot of sense to move on to a larger place. Three kids in one room just did not work anymore and a larger backyard was needed now as well. So, they were ready to sell and decided to do everything their agent suggested. Their agent complimented them on the inside of their home but said there were definitely some things to do on the outside to make the home have better curb appeal. There was a bit of stucco damage from a slight bump from the car right next to the garage. There were some shutters off kilter, and the door had some scuffing on the paint. They made a list and determined none of the work would cost much at all. In fact, the money involved was very, very minimal. They worked together and got things done, and they were amazed at the difference it made. There was definitely a whole lot more appeal from the curb! The work they put in worked, too. It was not long before they got an offer and then another. They did not get a third, though, because the house was already sold!

Tip: Oftentimes, very minor blemishes that do not impact your quality of life can nonetheless leave a bad impression with potential buyers. Here are some things to keep in mind.

1. A quick pressure wash of the driveway and walkways can make a bid difference in the appearance of the home.

2. Cleaning up the rain gutters can impact appearance beautifully.

3. Sometimes, all it takes is a little extra effort with minor repairs like cracked shutters or small stucco repairs.

LUCY AND LEWIS THINK ABOUT THE VIEW

Without question, the biggest selling point for Lucy and Lewis was the view. When they bought the home, they loved the sight from the backyard. Their agent said it was lovely but the problem was the front was not appealing so the chances of getting somebody to the backyard in order to look at the incredible view of the valley were very low. They needed to do something about that, but what? Their real estate agent suggested some tree trimming. If they got the trees under control, the view would be visible from the street. It would dramatically improve the curb appeal. They hired a tree trimming company and when the work was done they were surprised. From the street, the view of the valley almost called to them to take a closer look. They knew anyone interested in the home would have to get a better look, and that was exactly what they wanted in a first impression. Their agent was very happy and it was not long before they learned a happy agent meant offers coming in. It was hard to leave the view when their house sold but they knew they would love their new home.

Tip: Sometimes, a great selling point is not as obvious as it ought to be, and when that happens you should seriously consider what you can do to make it prominent. Here are some ideas.

1. Could moving a vehicle clear a path to a good view?

2. What can you do to highlight the home? Can you prune back some shrubs? Can you pull some smaller plants?

3. Remember the goal of curb appeal is to make the house as attractive as possible from the street. What will that take?

For Sale by Owner

HARLEY AND MOLLY SELL THEIR HOME

The offer surprised them. It was just above the asking price but it also included the owners carrying back a portion of the purchase price as a note. A friend told them that often happened when a person did a "for sale by owner" sale. They thought about it and discussed the possibilities. They had enough equity in the home to manage it, and the idea of monthly income coming from the note payments was actually very attractive. They had to work with the title company in order to have a note they were confident met the legal requirements, and they also wanted to make sure the deed of trust was done correctly. At closing, they felt excited to know they had helped someone get into a home and they not only got a good bit of cash from the process but also had monthly payments they would receive. On the whole, they thought it was a wild success. They received payments for four years and then the new owner refinanced. Everything work out well, and they were thankful they got the offer with an owner carry in the first place!

Tip: If you are going to try to sell your home yourself, here are some important thoughts to keep in mind.

1. When an agent is not involved, buyers who enjoy "creative" transactions feel more free to make offers.

2. Often, selling with an "owner carry" option can be a very significant selling point but you will want to research the impacts and speak with a tax professional.

3. Remember you have recourse if your buyer does not pay but the process can be long and laborious.

HARRISON AND EMMA DO IT THEMSELVES

They did not really decide they did not want an agent so much as they just started working on selling their home. Harrison was a website designer so he put together a lovely website. Emma was a graphic designer so signs and online advertisements were easy for her. She was excited to get moving and happy with the interest that almost immediately was shown. Of course, they had a little bit of help. Emma's best friend was a very successful real estate agent and she told Emma some of the pitfalls they might want to consider. That help was invaluable to them, and it gave them the confidence to approach the sale with gusto. The work was not easy but they really enjoyed it, and really loved that they were taking control of their own destiny. They knew for sale by owner was not for everyone but if there one thing they knew above all else, it was definitely for them. They were excited when they chose an offer and entered escrow, and they felt like they learned a great deal about buying and selling real estate in the process. In fact, when it was all over, Emma had serious thoughts about maybe becoming a real estate agent herself!

Tip: Real estate agents market your home but they also handle management of the sale process as well so you will want to consider a few things.

1. You will need a sale contract that is legal and enforceable in your state.

2. In order to offer title insurance to your buyer, you will need to have a title officer to help you.

3. If you are unfamiliar with certain real estate terms, you may want to pick up a book so you can negotiate with understanding.

HUNTER AND VIOLET DECIDE TO TRY

The two of them were always known as do-it-yourself folks, so it was no surprise to their friends that when they decided to sell their home they decided to do it themselves. Of course, selling your home was not the same as building a deck! They had a lot of research to do because they wanted to make sure everything was done correctly. Hunter focused on the procedural aspects, how the home sale would actually progress. Violet focused on the legal implications, including what paperwork would have to be put in place to keep the sale completely above board. It got very complicated very fast, and they did not feel entirely confident about the situation. They were nothing if not dedicated, though, so they started but agreed they would hire an agent if they needed one. The truth was, there was a whole lot of work to the process and there was plenty of disappointment, too. They imagined they had expected for there to be offers the moment they decided to sell. Of course it did not work out that way but they were committed and kept working and when the home sold, they could not say if it was better that they did it themselves but they could say they were happy with the final result.

Tip: When you sell your home without an agent, a great many people will interpret that as an excuse to make complicated offers. Keep this in mind.

1. Sometimes, people who would have trouble buying a home traditionally will take advantage of the opportunity to get creative in a FSBO situation.

2. In a FSBO situation, it is usually best to stick to an uncomplicated standard purchase agreement and transaction.

3. Remember that people earn their living as real estate agents. This is because there is a great deal of work involved in transactions. You can probably sell without an agent but there is a great deal involved in the process.

JAKE AND LUNA SELL BY OWNER

They knew they would feel better once the signs were all up and there were a number of advertisements online. Jake and Luna felt a little bit excited but they also felt a lot of trepidation. Were they doing the right thing? If they did the job poorly, they certainly would not save any money from agent commission. In fact, they might lose money! After letting themselves panic for a little bit, they finally laughed. After all, if they ended up in over their heads they could hire an agent to help them later. That pushed them over the edge. They had to get started or they might never do it. They did not want to get caught up in analysis paralysis. They wanted to at least make the biggest effort they could, and that meant getting started. Jake gave Luna a kiss and then went outside to set up the two for sale by owner signs. Luna put the sign in the front window right next to the door. There would be a great deal of work to do, they were sure, but what they knew more than anything else was that they would do everything they could to make the experience wonderful, not just successful. Hey, if there was a great deal of work in the process, they might as well really enjoy the ride, right?

Tip: There are legal implications in the sale of a home so if you do not have an agent to guide you, you will want to keep some things in mind.

1. Even in a for sale by owner situation, making a deal with an agent to ensure the paperwork is in order might be a good idea.

2. Make sure you understand the process so that when the sale occurs it can be handled properly.

3. If things are not working out, do not think of it as failure. If you decide to use an agent later, it just means you are committed to a successful transaction.

JAXON AND AMBER CONSIDER THEIR OPTIONS

Three offers already! Jaxon and Amber had no idea they would be so successful trying to sell their home by themselves. Of course, it was a little scary because they did not want to make any mistakes with the process. Jaxon suggested they call Amber's sister. Amber knew Sonia would tease her about it but she had to admit it was a very good idea. After all, Sonia was a very successful real estate agent up North. She would be able to give them some pointers. There was no doubt about that. Amber laughed because she knew Sonia would act like all the success was hers! That was okay. She called her sister and then faxed the offers over. As predicted, when Sonia got them on the phone, she certainly enjoyed that she was the expert. Amber rolled her eyes a lot but she had to admit when they hung up the phone that Sonia had been a big help. They set two of the offers aside and fashioned a counter offer for the third. After Sonia looked at the counter offer, they presented it to the buyer and the buyer accepted! They were as happy as could be and as Jaxon ordered a big bouquet of flowers for Sonia, Amber said she would never live the situation down but it was worth it.

Tip: Remember that if you decide to sell your home yourself, you will need to be available to your potential buyers and may end up in uncomfortable situations!

1. While an agent is expected to be available to show your home, your boss might not be happy with you leaving in the morning!

2. A real estate agent is required to share with you every single offer that arrives but an agent can also put those offers in context. In a FSBO situation, you do not have the advantage of an explanation.

3. Even if you are selling yourself, it is critical that you reach out for help or information when you need it.

JOSEPH AND LOTTIE AND FOR SALE BY OWNER

Lottie was the one who suggested they sell the home themselves. They were both investors so they were certain they had the experience and knowledge necessary. It did not take long before they realized how complicated the process was. They had to figure out what to do and they had to figure it out quickly. Jake was about ready to just hire an agent and Lottie agreed but then Jake came across a friend who had succeeded and they decided to give it a shot. They enjoyed a wonderful dinner with Tom and Linda and learned a lot about everything the two of them had done. Armed with that information, they had signs made and got the house advertised on a number of websites. It did not take long before people began to show interest, and it was not too long after that before they received an offer they really liked. Tom explained they should hire an escrow company to take care of the transaction so they did. When the house closed, they were absolutely thrilled. Jake and Linda could not have been happier, and when they moved into the near home, they wanted to celebrate a little. Of course, they took Tom and Linda out to a fancy restaurant to thank them for their help. They felt wonderful and it was great to know they had friends they could rely on for something so important.

Tip: Be sure of yourself when you sell your home. You worked hard to buy it and you deserve to manage the process of selling it.

1. Remember selling your home without an agent generally keeps you from using the multiple listing service, one of the most powerful sales tools.

2. A written marketing plan is usually a very good idea. Writing it down helps you crystalize ideas and also hold yourself accountable.

3. Legal ownership of a home is accomplished with a deed/title transfer. An escrow company or a title company is the safest way to accomplish that.

JUDE AND DARCIE THINK THEY CAN HANDLE IT

When their church decided to move to a new property, Jude was on the committee handling the sale and Darcie was on the committee handling the purchase. They learned a great deal about the process as the church moved to a new location and they had to handle two very large, condition-laden purchases. When it was all done, Jude and Darcie celebrated with a nice dinner out. They had performed a great service for the church and they could feel very good about that. While they celebrated, Darcie said if they could endure the complicated things they had just gone through; perhaps it was time to make the move they had talked about for years. All of their children were out of the house now and two of the three had ended up in the same town two states away. They had planned at some point to move there to be closer to the grandchildren. Now that they had some experience, they decided to go for it. They discovered there were a great many things about selling a home that were different than when a commercial property was sold but they had a lot of motivation—the smiling faces of their sweet grandkids! Jude and Darcie thought about all the barbecues and family dinners they would enjoy. It was going to be wonderful.

Tip: Remember that there are multiple kinds of buyers and you cannot necessarily target your home to all of them at once.

1. Sometimes, the quickest sale will be a sale to an investor who will either flip your home or resell it.

2. Sometimes the home is appropriate as a "starter" home, a home that is usually smaller and more affordable than other homes in the area.

3. Remember that experience in one kind of sale does not necessarily translate to other situations.

LOUIE AND GEORGIA HAVE SOME TIME

Louie's promotion had just gone through but he had three months to report to his new office four states away. As for Georgia, she had just completed her novel and had time as well. This, more than anything, was the reason they decided that they would try to sell their home without the help of an agent. After all, they had three whole months. How hard could it be? They learned pretty quickly it could be difficult. In fact, four months later, Georgia was still at the old home trying to sell it while Louie was alone at their new home, working at the new office and settling into his new job. They decided they needed to hire an agent after all and that was what they did. Louie felt a bit like a failure over the whole situation. After all, he was admitting defeat was he not? Of course, when Georgia finally got out to their new home, those feelings went away. After all, the goal was to get the home sold and to be together as they built their lives in the new location. That was not about ego and it certainly was not about who actually accomplished the sale!

Tip: If you are going to sell your home and not involve an agent, you will want to do some research to determine some important things about the sale.

1. You will want to know what similar homes in your area have sold for and are currently priced.

2. You will really need to manage your expectations. Sales of homes can take a great deal of time. The purchases are significant.

3. Most importantly, do not forget that you can hire an agent whenever you need to do so. It does not make you a failure to accept that you need help.

LUCA AND ELIZABETH DO NOT SELL BY OWNER

Elizabeth felt like paying an agent was a waste of money. Luca thought it would be money well spent but they compromised. They would try to sell without an agent but if they did not make any progress, they would hire an agent. That seemed like fair to both of them and they worked hard on the sale. Elizabeth spent more time in the process than Luca because Luca's job made him travel a great deal while Elizabeth had a lot more flexibility in that regard. In the process of trying to sell the home, Elizabeth learned a great deal about real estate. In fact, she began to consider investing in property once things were complete with the sale. When she talked to Luca about it, she explained all the reasons she thought it was a great idea. Luca was convinced. In fact, he was so convinced he suggested they do not sell their home. They could afford to buy a new home while keeping this one and it would be a good way to get started on being a property investor. So, they took the house off the market and instead searched for a renter. They had not expected things to work out that way but they were happy they did.

Tip: Remember when you sell as an owner that you need to keep on top of the sale process. Think about some of these things.

1. One of the wonderful things about a for sale by owner process is that if you are diligent about things you are very likely to learn a great deal that may be helpful to you in the future.

2. Sometimes, it may make sense to keep a home you plan to sell. Of course, you will want to make sure you do not need access to the equity in the home and you will want to make sure the rent can cover the mortgage payment.

3. Compromise is often critical when making property decisions with your significant other.

REGGIE AND ZARA AND THEIR FSBO HOME

When Zara got promoted, she and Reggie realized they would finally be able to move out of their starter home and get their dream home. They were excited and so were the kids! The promotion included a very, very sizable bonus. In addition, their years of frugal living meant they had a great deal in savings as well. They realized they could buy the dream home without having to worry about when the starter home would sell. With that in mind, they made their offer and were thrilled when it was accepted. It was not until they were fully moved in that they thought about what to do with their first home. Their seventeen year old daughter had really considered getting into real estate as a career so they decided it would be a good experience for her if they sold the home themselves and gave her a lot of exposure to what was involved. It took almost a year for the home to sell but they did not mind. They especially did not mind when their daughter got a great job with a real estate firm and being an agent put her through college and graduate school! To think it all started from a for sale by owner situation! Years later, when their daughter had her own brokerage firm, they would often laugh about that first experience but most importantly, they would look back on it all with a great deal of fondness.

Tip: Do not forget that you will need the help of some professionals whether or not you hire a real estate agent. Here are a few you may require.

1. Title company/escrow company. Most buyers will want title insurance, and that means you will need to involve professionals.

2. Home inspectors. Most buyers will want an inspection of the home, and that may be your responsibility.

3. Appraisers. Although the buyer will need to hire an appraiser for the financing, you may need to coordinate with them so they have access to the house.

Tales of Owner Financing

REUBEN AND PENELOPE CARRY THE NOTE

Reuben and Penelope had lived frugally in order to afford their starter home. They lived frugally in their starter home for eight years and still lived frugally as they raised their four children in their next home. Now, their frugal living had paid off. They owned their home free and clear. They were especially happy because their home was located perfectly in terms of the growth of the city, and it had appreciated very significantly since they bought it. In fact, their new home, just forty-five minutes away, would cost less than the home they were selling, and it had two more bedrooms that where they were! Everything seemed wonderful and most of their conversations were about how to make sure they celebrated but did not waste the money they had the good fortune to expect. So, when their agent said they received an offer with owner financing, they were in the right frame of mind to consider it. The buyers wanted a second mortgage, and that meant the bulk of the sale price would still come with cash. On the whole, it seemed like a great idea and they were happy with monthly payments. They gathered the kids together and told them they would be moving soon!

Tip: Remember that if you carry back a portion of the loan price, it will be secured by the home itself. This means a number of things.

1. Just like a bank, you have the right to foreclose on the home if your note is not paid. However, there is a legal process that must be followed.

2. If your note is a second note behind a first mortgage, keep in mind the first mortgage would always be paid first.

3. You will need to make sure your mortgage or deed of trust is recorded properly with the appropriate governmental agencies.

RILEY AND HOLLY OFFER A CARRY BACK

Riley and Holly decided to get into real estate note investing and they were very happy with the return. In fact, in twelve years they had earned enough that they almost owned their home free and clear. They decided to sell so each of the kids could have their own room. Since they had a lot of experience in note investments, they decided they would offer owner financing. It made more sense to them than renting their first house. Instead, they would finance with a sizable down payment and work what they already understood. Their agent had some good recommendations for them. He talked with them about the length of the note—how long the buyer would have to pay it off. He also talked about the interest rate as well as an amortization schedule. They were already familiar with the terms involved because of their previous investments but it was very helpful to speak to the agent in regards to what would be attractive to potential buyers. After the meeting, they felt even more confident and when the home sold and they enjoyed the view from the back porch of their new home, they decided they had definitely made the right decision. They would help a couple get into a home and they had a beautiful new house. They had payments that would come every month, and that was a wonderful thing as well. All in all, life was grand!

Tip: Owner financing comes in many forms. Here are some possibilities for you to consider.

1. First mortgage. Sometimes, you will handle all of the financing necessary on a home.

2. Second mortgage. Sometimes, the buyer will have financing and you will carry a second mortgage.

3. Interest only. Some owners finance as a sort of bridge loan, offering an interest only loan with a shorter term and a balloon payment.

RONNIE AND NANCY AND A SECOND MORTGAGE

Ronnie and Nancy did not expect an offer to include a request for owner financing. They were not opposed completely. They needed to cover their mortgage and they needed a certain amount they had planned for a down payment on their new home. The rest of the sale price was flexible so they could manage the financing the buyer requested. Of course, they had a great many questions for their agent. They did not know what paperwork was needed. They did not know what they would have to do at all, in fact. What would they do if the buyer did not make payments? What about the terms involved? Were they negotiable? Were they allowed to take a look at the buyer's income and credit history? That seemed like a pretty important step as well. Anyone watching would have thought they were opposed to the idea but the agent could tell Ronnie and Nancy were excited. He patiently answered all of their questions and before long, they issued a counter-offer to the buyer with slightly different terms on the note. They were thrilled when the buyer agreed and they were very thankful for the great help their agent offered.

Tip: Sometimes owner financing is the only way to save the deal. In those circumstances, you will want to consider a number of things.

1. What are the risks you assume when you agree to receive deferred compensation?

2. What would you do if the buyer did not make the mortgage payments and you had to undertake legal procedures to make it work?

3. You have the right to determine the creditworthiness of the buyer before you make a decision about owner financing.

RORY AND ROSE ARE WILLING TO DEAL

Rory and Rose found themselves in a bit of a quandary. They were receiving a great many offers but none of them were meeting their price goal. Their agent offered them a surprising idea. What if they considered an owner carry? That might attract more buyers and get them closer to their sale price goal. They were not opposed to that idea and decided to give it a shot. They worked with the agent on terms and when he updated the listing he told them he would also make counteroffers to some of the earlier offers and see if they got any takers. They figured they had nothing to lose so they decided to give it a shot. They were very thankful they followed their agent's advice, too, because they got two new offers and all of them met their price goals. They did not accept them, though, because one of the earlier buyers agreed to their price with an owner-carry second mortgage. Everything worked out and they would also get a small monthly payment they decided they would put right into their kids' college fund. All in all, their disappointment had turned into a wonderful opportunity for a real happy outcome. As far as Rory and Rose were concerned, that was perfect!

Tip: Some people invest in real estate notes as a business. Owner financing is a small foray into that world.

1. Remember if you offer either a first or second mortgage, you have security with the property.

2. When you are only carrying back a small portion of the purchase price, you may want to decide on a special goal for the monthly payments.

3. Remember than your agent has experience in a great many areas so you may want to make decisions after carefully considering their ideas.

SAMUEL AND EMILIA WILL CARRY BACK

When their agent told them about a potential offer, Samuel and Emilia were a bit surprised. The potential buyer wanted them to carry back a portion of the purchase price. They had not considered doing that. They had not thought about it at all before and their first inclination was to deny the offer but them Emilia looked at Sam and he recognized the look in her face. They decided to talk it over and then sleep on it. The next morning, they surprised their agent. They decided to accept the offer. For the two of them, it came down to a simple fact. They had plenty of equity and they had spent time trying to figure out what to do with the money they would get with the sale and had not been able to agree on a conclusion. The note had a balloon payment in two years and that was plenty of time for them to come up with a good way to spend or invest the proceeds. When they entered escrow, they were excited and when the home closed they were even more excited. Best of all, it was wonderful to talk about their future without a deadline pressing up against them. All in all, they thought the sale was a wonderful success!

Tip: Owner financing is just like other financing in terms of what is involved. Here are things to consider.

1. Term. Will the buyer pay you back over the course of a year? Five years? Ten years? Twenty?

2. Taxes. There may be tax implications and you will want to talk to a professional about that. In addition, there may be tax implications to a balloon payment later.

3. Payments. Will they be interest only? Will they be amortized with principal and interest so the loan is paid over a period of time?

SEBASTIAN AND HARRIET HAVE PLENTY OF EQUITY

Sebastian and Harriet looked forward to spending the rest of their lives travelling. They had both worked very hard and now that they were retiring, they planned to drive across the country visiting their children and grandchildren on an ongoing, never-ending tour. For them, that seemed absolutely perfect, and they had everything prepared. They were just tying up loose ends and selling the home they had owned free and clear for almost a decade was one of the loose ends they had to tie up. They already had their retirement accounts in very good shape and they imagined they would just bank the money from the sale. So, when their real estate agent told them they received an offer that included owner financing, they were very open to the idea. They thought the terms were fair, a mortgage amortized over twenty years with a fair interest rate. They thought the ongoing income would be great and they also imagined it would be easier in terms of taxes. They accepted the offer and just about a month later the home closed. They used the down payment money to buy a nice RV and hit the road. They could already hear the laughter of their grandkids and they could not imagine anything that could possibly sound better.

Tip: Like any other loan, owner financing has variations. Here are things to think about in regard to the note.

1. Will you amortize the loan or charge only interest with a balloon payment due after a period of time?

2. If you plan to finance the home in a primary position, how much of a down payment will you require?

3. If there are difficulties with the payments, how will you handle them? It would be better to make those kinds of decisions ahead of time than to be surprised by them.

THEODORE AND GRACIE ARE WILLING TO CARRY

When Theo and Gracie told their agent they were willing to sell the home with owner financing, she was surprised. That was usually a last resort kind of idea in her experience. They smiled and told her they had lived frugally for many years. This allowed them to send all three of their children to college and also to set aside money for their current future grandchildren. Not only did they own their home free and clear but they also had several income properties they rented out. Now that their oldest son had twins, they decided to move closer to help the family out. The point was, they did not need the money from the sale all at once and liked the idea of receiving monthly payments. Together with their agent, they worked out terms they liked. She helped them understand requiring a good down payment was a great idea because studies showed buyers with larger down payments tended to be better about making the monthly payments. They worked out an interest rate just slightly above the market. They could always come down if there was a counter offer. Their agent also let them know there were a great many companies and individual investors who actually purchased notes so they could sell the note at some point if they wanted to. When they were done with the terms, they were thrilled. They were certain things would work out wonderfully.

Tip: Some people choose to sell their note to an investor rather than manage the payments themselves. Keep some things in mind.

1. Just like with any other loan, risk is the key. If someone buys your note, the risk will impact the price.

2. There are many companies and individuals that will buy your note and the purchase price will have everything to do with the risk involved.

3. In some states, when a note is sold, it is automatically perfected. That means it is beyond challenge in terms of title.

TOMMY AND DARCY CARRY A PORTION

Tommy's tax attorney suggested she and Darcy sell their home, which they owned outright, with owner financing. The home had appreciated so much that there would be a very severe tax burden. So, they were faced with a choice of immediately transferring the money they earned into an investment property, offering owner financing or another installment sale, or just taking the tax hit. They knew they would still get some cash because of a homeowners' capital gain exception but they were still looking at having to pay almost one-hundred thousand in taxes. The tax attorney said if they offered an owner financing transaction, the down payment would easily fall within the exemption. They thought it made sense to follow their attorney's advice and that was how their listing included the owner carry. Of course, there was plenty of work to do. The owner carry nature of the situation seemed to bring out a great many buyers but most of them were not qualified for a loan and it seemed foolish to give them an owner carry. Finally, though, they received an offer they liked and in short order their home was sold. It seemed like the very best outcome, and Tommy and Darcy were thrilled when the house closed. They could move on and their attorney had protected them in a wonderful way.

Tip: There may be some legal and tax implications to owner financing and you will want to learn about them. Here are things to consider.

1. In many states, if your sell with a note, you are liable for taxes over a period of time as the note is paid instead of all at once like a cash transaction.

2. You do NOT want to make these kinds of decisions without the advice of a tax professional.

3. Remember to consider the difference between a deferral and an exemption. An exemption frees you from a tax obligation. A deferral allows you to pay the obligation later.

BLAKE AND ORLA CARRY BACK

Orla and Blake had not really considered owner financing but they owned their home free and clear. In fact, they owned three homes free and clear. They certainly did not need to receive all the money at one time. When their agent presented the offer he had received, it included a first mortgage owner carry of fifty percent of the value of the home. They were used to getting money monthly from a great many renters. Would it not be a similar thing to get money monthly as a note payment from the person who bought their home? They were also very happy with the fifty percent down payment. They knew that provided them with a great deal of security and they also knew it indicated that the buyer meant business. They decided to accept the offer and they were glad they did. By the time they were moved into their new house and really settled, they received the first payment. It was wonderful, and they thought about all the possibilities. They knew how to purchase properties and how to make deals. Maybe they could buy a bunch of houses and offer them with owner financing. The possibilities were endless. For now, though, Blake and Orla just loved that they were happy, really happy.

Tip: Do not be afraid to ask questions if a buyer you like asks for owner financing. Here are some things to keep in mind.

1. It is perfectly reasonable for you to want to understand the buyer's credit history and income if they want you to owner-finance.

2. A large down payment does two things. First, it makes the buyer more committed. Second, it gives you more security because the home's value is that much greater than the amount of the note.

3. Remember that if the buyer defaults, you will need to take action to protect your interest in the property.

STANLEY AND JASMINE AND THE OWNER CARRY

They certainly were not opposed to the idea. When their agent presented the offer to them, they realized there might even be some advantage to carrying a note. After all, they had not planned to spend the proceeds from the sale on anything in particular. They had not even planned to sell the home. It was an income property and they had owned it for years. When their long term renter told them they were moving, they decided to just put the home on the market. The idea of owner financing was unplanned as well but they were happy with the idea. They would receive monthly payments and that was a whole lot like what had happened for a number of years renting the property. They wanted to make sure the buyer could handle the cost of financing because they did not want to be stuck in a situation where they had to involve themselves in collection activity. Their agent suggested they ask for a credit report on the buyer. The buyer furnished one. The credit was not wonderful but it was not horrible. They decided to accept the offer and give the buyer a chance. After all, many years before someone gave them a chance. It felt nice to give back a little bit.

Tip: Owner financing is not reaching into your pocket to give someone a loan but it has the same effect. Consider these things.

1. There is always the possibility of default, so be aware that you may have to engage in collection activity.

2. Most people who seek owner financing do so because they cannot necessarily obtain traditional financing. Be aware of that.

3. The decision to carry a note is ultimately up to you. Listen to any advice you receive but remember the decision is yours.

Special Selling Situations

AARON AND ANNA AND THE UNIQUE SITUATION

When their real estate agent explained it to them, Aaron and Anna could not believe it. They had two pieces of property? They always thought they just had a double lot! It turned out their land was not just twice the size of the other lots in the neighborhood but was two separate lots right next to each other. The neighborhood was very popular and land in the area was actually the bulk of a purchase. The extra lot itself was worth almost seventy percent of the lot with the house on it! For Aaron and Anna, it felt like they had won the lottery. They briefly considered building another home on that lot but when it came right down to it, they had already been given a remarkable windfall and it seemed to them they would rather take advantage of it as is. They were not surprised that the lot sold much faster than their home but the house sold very quickly, too. They were thrilled. They could not believe how everything seemed to just work out for them, and they never would have known if they had not decided to sell the house. It just goes to show that sometimes wonderful things happen just because someone is diligent!

Tip: Often, there are real opportunities you might not expect that you only discover when you are in the process of selling. If you end up with an extra lot here are some thoughts for you.

1. You will need to check with your city planning department to see what restrictions and requirements exist that might impact the value.

2. You may decide to improve the lot by building on it prior to sale. You will want to make sure of permits in those cases as well.

3. Seek the advice of a professional to help you determine the right decision.

CONNOR AND SUMMER AND THE SURPRISING OFFER

When the offer came in, Connor and Summer were very surprised. Their agent explained to them what the offer meant and they were still surprised. The buyer wanted to buy their house but only if he could get certain permits approved by the city planning department. He was willing to pay for the process. It all seemed very complicated and they had no idea how long it would take. The agent explained he wanted to get approval for the addition of a second floor. After, he would close escrow. The agent suggested putting a time limit in place to keep the buyers on track. They wondered what would happen if they went through the process and then the buyer did not close. Would they not have gone through all that effort for nothing? The agent suggested that since the buyer would pay for the fees and the designs, it would cost them nothing but a little time and if they failed to close, the home would be worth more at that point anyway. That made the offer pretty attractive and Connor and Summer decided to go ahead with the deal. They were glad they did. Things went exactly as planned. Summer had to admit there were times she almost hoped the buyer would not close but now they had some experience with permitting and Connor was pretty sure they would be adding a room or two to their next home.

Tip: There are many different ways transactions in real estate occur. Here are a few things you might experience.

1. Owner financing. This is probably the most common special situation. Many buyers would rather have the owner finance than obtain traditional financing.

2. Property improvements. Sometimes this is just permitting or other civil work but sometimes it could include adding a driveway or another constructed element.

DEXTER AND ROBYN NEVER THOUGHT ABOUT THAT

Dexter and Robyn loved their land but they did not love their house all that much. It certainly met their needs when they bought it seven years before but now they had outgrown it. They got in touch with a real estate agent and he opened their eyes to an idea they had not considered. They had almost five acres but the land was zoned for up to four homes per acre. The agent said if they subdivided, they would be able to sell the house and sell the lots. They were likely to make a great deal more money that way. That was exciting but what Dexter and Robyn loved was that they could keep a portion of the land and build a home in the neighborhood they already loved. They really had not considered it but they went about the process. They subdivided the land so they had two acres all to themselves and started building. The rest of the land yielded another ten lots in addition to their current house, and they put those lots on the market right away. Before long, all ten were under construction and when their home was finished and they listed their starter house, they were amazed to discover that the value of the home had actually increased because of how much the neighborhood improved with the new construction. It was a wonderful success and they were absolutely grateful to the real estate agent who showed them the possibilities!

Tip: Sometimes, an opportunity arises in the midst of a real estate transaction that you might not have expected. When that occurs, you will want to rely on the help of your agent. Here are some thoughts.

1. When you think of a land subdivision project, you probably think of dozens of lots or more. It can actually be as few as two.

2. Subdividing land does not require you to actually build homes in most cases. You can sell the land to contractors, developers and individuals.

3. A number of new homes in a neighborhood will often result in an increase in the value of all the homes in that neighborhood.

DOMINIC AND LEXI ARE OPEN TO THE IDEA

When the buyer asked about a lease with an option to buy, Dominic and Lexi gave it a lot of thought. They had already closed on their new home. So, they did not need to get a large cash payoff. The mortgage payment was very manageable, even if the tenant was slow to pay. Their agent explained a lease-option was essentially the same as renting. However, the tenants would also pay a fee to have the right to buy the house at a specified time in the future. When they asked what would happen if the family could not complete the purchase later, they learned they would have options at that point that could include extending the time frame or could include ending the option and not renewing the lease. It seemed like a good plan to Dominic and Lexi and they decided to give it a shot. It worked out very well. Nine months later, the buyers exercised their option and in the meantime, they had received the rents. They actually started buying investment properties to enter into lease to own contracts with potential buyers. They loved the success and they also loved that they could help people out who might need to rebuild their credit or have some time to generate their down payment.

Tip: Sometimes it might make sense to involve yourself in a sale transaction that is not run of the mill. Here are some thoughts.

1. Lease to own. Sometimes, you can rent a home to a tenant who also purchases an option to buy the home.

2. Land sales. In these cases, buyers make payments but do not get title to the home until the last payments are completed.

3. Always seek legal advice so when you enter into a contract you are fully protected.

ELI AND HEIDI HIT THE JACKPOT

Who would have thought their home was worth more than they could have imagined? Eli and Heidi were both creative types, and they really had not paid much attention to the housing market over the decade they owned their home. Appreciation meant they had twice as much equity in the home as they owed on their mortgage. They had not planned on selling but when they learned of the value of their home it seemed like a good idea. For years they had wanted to move back to their hometown. They wanted to be inspired by the rural sunsets and beautiful days to really develop Heidi's musical career and Eli's painting career. With the value of the house, they could buy their new home with cash. They hired a real estate agent and called their families to tell them the great news. When the offer came in, they were really surprised. It was for a significantly higher amount than the asking price as long as they were able to move right away. With the extra money, they would have plenty left over to add a painting studio for Eli and a music studio for Heidi. They could move quickly, too, because they could stay with either set of parents while they decided on a home. They were so happy to be going home. They would be close to the friends they had grown up with and, of course, they would get the chance to spend a lot more time with family. It was like a dream come true for these creative geniuses!

Tip: Sometimes buyers are very motivated and willing to go above and beyond in order to meet their particular goals and needs.

1. Sometimes, buyers have a great deal of urgency and in order to affect a fast close, they are willing to pay a higher purchase price.

2. In some cases, buyers get into a bidding "war" for the home, each increasing the offer in order to be the one who gets the house.

3. Sometimes, an area appreciates so quickly in value that prices go up with every week you have it on the market.

ELLIOT AND ANNABELLE SELL WITH PURPOSE

When Annabelle went to college, she moved into her grandmother's house. Seven years later, her grandmother passed away and left the house to her. When she got her doctorate degree, she dedicated it to the granny she loved. Now, she and her husband had three children and the house she loved was just too small for them. They decided to sell and that was when Annabelle learned something amazing. The home was actually in a city zone that allowed commercial property, residential property or mixed use property. She knew there were a lot of little offices in front of homes on the street but she had no idea that was a zoning issue. She was surprised when she learned that the zoning made the value of her home higher than if the land was just residential. So, the home would actually be listed at a price almost thirty percent higher than she and her husband had anticipated. She was surprised but it was, of course, a wonderful surprise. Now, they would be able to make a much larger down payment on their new home or maybe set aside some money for the kids' college fund. It was amazing how many options seemed to open up for them. As she signed the listing paperwork, she smiled at her husband, who was occupying the kids in the front room where they played. In the new house, they would have a playroom and a much bigger backyard. Life was really and truly beautiful.

Tip: Often, learning about your property will tell you the best way to sell. Here are some things you can consider.

1. Are there legal or civil opportunities such as zoning or permitting privileges?

2. Is your land large enough that you can have it split into an extra lot or two?

3. Has your house appreciated over the years? When was the last time you tried to determine your home's value?

ELLIS AND MARIA SELL THE BACKYARD

When Ellis and Maria first bought their home, the biggest selling point was the back yard. It was very, very big. In fact, it was so big they put a gate on the back fence and were able to drive their cars in from the street behind them. They had no idea the reason the yard was so big because it was actually another residential lot. They found out when a real estate agent approached them and said there was a buyer interested in the lot. At first, they refused. They loved their home and wanted to stay there for many, many years. The agent explained the buyer only wanted the lot behind theirs. That was when they learned it was a separate property. It even had its own parcel number from the tax assessor. They were so surprised they went over the paperwork from when they bought the home years before. Sure enough, there were two lot numbers on the paperwork. How had they missed that? Part of their surprise, of course, was that the lot was very valuable. In fact, they would have imagined a lot could not sell for that much without having a home on top of it! Their backyard would not be as big but it still seemed like the right decision and they went through with the sale. A year later as they enjoyed iced tea on the back porch and watched the kids playing football in their smaller but still perfect backyard, they were sure it was the right thing to do.

Tip: Often, opportunities arrive about which you had no idea prior to the transaction. Here are some possibilities.

1. Sometimes, a unique situation, like an over-sized backyard, should be investigated for more opportunity.

2. Sometimes a zoning change gives your property more potential opportunity and that can impact the value.

3. Sometimes opportunities arise by accident. Just be open to the possibilities.

GABRIEL AND AURORA DO NOT HAVE TO PACK

They had not advertised their home as furnished so Gabriel and Aurora were a little surprised when the offer came in and included all of the furniture. Their agent said it was not all that uncommon and she had dealt with it before. Since they had planned to replace a lot of their furniture with the proceeds from the sale, they did not really mind. In fact, since the offer was a few thousand dollars higher than their asking price because of the addition of the furniture, they would actually end up ahead on the deal. What more could they ask for? They agreed to the deal except for one antique chest they needed to keep. It was a family heirloom from the late 1800s, and there was no way Aurora could even imagine giving up the mahogany inlaid chest. She had wonderful memories of sitting on that chest and listening to stories from her grandmother! The agent said not to worry and made it clear to the buyer's agent that the sale would not include the chest. The buyers did not mind at all and so the deal was done. Later, in their new home, they sat happily on their new sofa and smiled at how everything worked out. Of course, the antique chest was right where it belonged at the foot of Aurora's new bed!

Tip: Purchasing some of the non-real estate property at a home is not as uncommon as you might think. Here are some thoughts.

1. Often, a buyer's loan will pay for the extra purchases which is why it can be attractive to someone who has used all of their savings for a down payment.

2. It is appropriate for the price to increase in relation to the additional value the buyer is receiving.

3. Remember to account for how not having the items included in the sale might impact you. It can be easy to forget, for example, that you need to get a new refrigerator before you move in.

GRAYSON AND LEAH AND THE SPECIAL SALE

Grayson and Leah could not understand why the buyer would not budge about the guest house. He would buy the home but only if the guest house got new flooring. They could not understand why switching from carpet to tile was so important to the buyer and why something that would only cost a few thousand dollars held up a million dollar sale. Leah told Grayson they should just do it. Grayson was adamant the buyer was being unreasonable, though. Finally, their agent took action. He learned the buyer intended the guest house for her grandmother. He also learned she had a very bad breathing problem and carpet could be dangerous because it trapped dirt and dust. Finally, he learned that the buyer's brother was a contractor but not a very good one. If she bought the house, she would be expected to use him to fix the floors. If, on the other hand, the floors were already fixed there would be no family drama. Grayson admitted to Leah he had indeed been stubborn and they agreed to the terms. A month and a half later, the home closed and they were glad they had enjoyed the opportunity to help the buyer.

Tip: The best real estate agents will try to under-stand the motivations of buyers and sellers and cre-ate win/win situations. Here are some thoughts.

1. When you do not understand the motivations of the buyer, you will not know how to ap-proach them.

2. When you learn the buyer's needs and motiva-tions, you are in a better position to make the transaction work.

3. This is all part of what your real estate agent should provide for you and it is not wrong of you to expect this level of action.

JAMIE AND DARCEY AND THEIR FIRST INVESTMENT

Sometimes, what makes a sale a special situation is how the proceeds will be used. Jamie and Darcey were excited because they were moving back to their home town. One of the great things about that, other than being really close to family, was that they would live in an area where the housing prices were far lower. In fact, they planned to use the proceeds from their sale to buy a much nicer home in the home town as well one or two more as income properties. They were really excited about the prospect and, frankly, Darcey was excited that they were going back to run her family business. Her parents were retiring, and she loved that Jamie was willing to go back to keep the business in the family. Jamie was very excited. He knew how important the business was to Darcey and he knew his experience in business was going to be a big help. They hired an agent and told her they were motivated sellers. They wanted to sell quickly and they wanted to get to the next phase of their life. The agent was glad to help and told him they would list the property at market value but indicate they would entertain all offers. That did the trick. In just a day an offer came in below the asking price. They accepted the offer and smiled because they would soon be back home.

Tip: Often, people discover they have a great deal of equity in their home. Sometimes, they refinance but sometimes they sell. Here are some ideas.

1. There are likely tax consequences to a sale, and you should consult with a professional to understand them.

2. If you are motivated to move to your new home quickly and you have the resources to accept a smaller price, you should let your agent know.

3. If you do not want to move and decide to re-finance, remember you need to make sure you can afford the mortgage payments.

More Stories about Selling

NANCY AND PAUL DECIDE TO SELL

The bottom line, as far as Nancy was concerned, was that it no longer made sense for them to live in their starter house. She remembered fondly how much she and Paul had celebrated when they bought it but that was four years and two children ago. They needed a bigger home, and more importantly they needed a home closer to Paul's office. Nancy worked from home so anywhere with an internet connection worked for her but she wanted Paul to be able to work without forty-five minutes on the road each way. So, the sale had to happen. There were just no two ways about it. She was bittersweet about the whole thing but more than anything she wanted to do the right thing for her family and the right thing was a new house. To make that work, they would need to sell the old home, no matter how much they loved the house. Sure, life would be wonderful if they could keep it and still get the new house but part of moving forward in life was leaving some things behind. She and Paul would sell, and it would be wonderful thing when they moved into their new house. She knew it would work out wonderfully but more than anything, she knew everyone was going to be very happy with the new place.

Tip: When you would like to sell a home to move to a home in the same area that better meets your needs, here are a few tips to consider.

1. Consider having your selling agent also handle finding you the home to which you will move. You will have an agent very motivated with both ends of the deal.

2. Remember to consider how long you want to live in the new home. Are you planning on having more kids? Are you planning on getting a pet?

3. Sometimes, selling a house can feel just like leaving home. Cherish the memories you made there but commit yourself to making more.

HAL AND VICKY FIND AN AGENT

Hal and Vicky were at their wits' end. They just felt like none of the agents vying for their business actually cared about how they felt. They could not remember a time when they had felt so much pressure in sales! Hal felt ready to just throw up his hands and take care of things himself. He and Vicky might have done just that if an agent had not shown up who was different from all the others. Instead of telling, this agent asked questions. It was almost shocking. Instead of talking about what the property was worth or what they might get, he asked what it was they wanted to accomplish. They thought that was amazing. It was like the agent actually cared about them. It was all so refreshing after all of the other interviews. Hal and Vicky were excited and eager to see what the agent would do. They signed the listing agreement and, sure enough, they were very pleased with all of the work he did. It did not take too long before they received an offer and then another. They were excited, and they were especially excited because every step of the way they felt like they were being treated exactly like they would treat their friends and family.

Tip: More than anything, you need an agent who is willing to listen to your needs. When you talk to an agent, pay attention to a few things.

1. Does the agent spend more time asking questions to understand your needs or asking questions to get you to agree to things?

2. Does the agent seem sincere about listening to what you have to say?

3. Does the agent give careful consideration to your questions and does the agent provide thoughtful responses?

JESSIE AND HALLIE MAKE THINGS WORK

Jessie and Hallie felt pretty unhappy. They had gone a whole year and the home did not sell. The listing expired and they were so tired about things they did not want to bother with the sale anymore. In fact, Jessie's company offered to extend her contract for a year and she was pretty sure that was the right decision. Hallie was disappointed with that idea because she knew how much Jessie wanted to move back to her home town. She suggested they at least interview a few agents and see if any of the new possibilities impressed them. Jessie did not have a lot of confidence but she agreed to at least give it a try. They interviewed some agents but neither of them had much hope. There was one agent who at least seemed very enthusiastic so they decided to give her a try. They were very pleasantly surprised by the agent's actions. First of all, she kept in constant contact and even gave them a list of suggestions to make the house more attractive, suggestions like yardwork and rearranging the front room furniture. After a month, they started to allow themselves hope. When the offers started coming in, they realized their hopes were well-founded. A few months later, when they arrived in their new home, Hallie knew it was all worth it just by the happy look on Jessie's face.

Tip: Often, just a small change in outlook is all it takes to make a successful sale. Here are some ideas for you.

1. Do not give up! The key is to think in terms of different actions, different things you can do to reach your goals.

2. Sometimes, a real estate agent is not a good fit for you. When a listing expires, it makes sense to ask a potential new agent what they plan to do differently to sell your home.

KAI AND MARTHA DECIDE ON ACTION

If there was one thing Kai and Martha knew, it was that they could not keep doing the same thing and expect to get different results. They had been talking about moving closer to Kai's family for four years but it seemed like they never took the next step. One evening after dinner the subject came up again and right in the middle of it, Martha said they should just face facts. They talked about it all the time but they were never actually going to move. The statement was shocking but it had a wonderful effect. The two of them talked seriously about how important it was to them. They decided right then and there that they needed to take action. That meant now and not later. Kai pulled up some potential real estate agents on his phone and they left six messages. Then, they checked home prices in their target area and were surprised because the cost for a home by Martha's family was far less expensive than where they currently lived. The next day, the agents began calling back. They interviewed three and gave one the listing. They had made the first step, and Kai and Martha knew it would not be too long before they were living in a new town. More importantly, they knew they had taken a very important step, the first one!

Tip: Selling a home can be a very big decision. Here are some things to consider if you are on the fence about it.

1. Think about afterward. What will you do if you sell the home? What will you do if you do not sell the home?

2. Sometimes, our tendency to stay in the same situation is stronger than our motivation to act. Overcoming inertia can be a difficult thing but it is worth it!

3. You have heard the cliché about a journey beginning with a single step. It may be trite and cliché but it is also true!

LEON AND AMELIE DO IT RIGHT

Leon and Amelie knew nothing at all about real estate and they knew that meant they would have to rely on whomever they hired to sell the home for them. The problem was that Leon and Amelie both had a great deal of business experience and both of them were used to being heavily involved in every aspect of the business. Some might call them micromanagers. They knew they could be overbearing but they also knew a home sale was important enough that they would not be able to just let someone else handle it without involving them. Leon suggested when they interview agents they would need to make sure they understood the two of them would be heavily involved. Amelie agreed. They made some calls and set some appointments. It was very important to them that they could be involved and they wanted that clear from the outset. Two of the agents with whom they met seemed a bit taken aback but the third agent nodded as they spoke and said she would be happy to make sure they were with her every step of the way. With that, she outlined her marketing plan and the actions she intended to take to make the sale happen. They thought that was a very good start and over the four following months, right up until the house closed and they received the sale proceeds, the agent kept her word. They got to be involved every step of the way.

Tip: When you hire a real estate agent, you are hiring expertise. Think very hard about who you hire but then make sure you follow the advice they give.

1. Try to get referrals, customers who have used them in the past. Ask specifically to talk to a customer who might be less than satisfied.

2. Tell your agent what you expect. This may be a weekly update or it may be a daily update. Communicate before you list the home so that the experience works for you.

3. Remember you are paying your agent. In some cases, you are paying a tremendous amount. You deserve an agent who takes your requirements seriously!

LIAM AND KATIE MAKE THE MOVE

Of course Liam and Katie were overjoyed about her promotion but there were a lot of things that needed to happen. Liam's work was not a problem. His position allowed him to work remotely so that would be seamless. The real issue was that they were still young in their careers. They could not afford the new house until the old house sold. The agent in the city where they would move told them he could make offers contingent on the sale of their first home. The real issue was that Katie would have to report to the new location soon. Her company was paying for relocation but they still needed to deal with the sale of their house. They knew the house they owned now was worth far more than the one they would be buying. The real issue at the moment, though, was time. Tentatively, they asked if they could possibly get a long escrow on the house they wanted to buy. The agent presented the offer to the seller and the seller accepted. They were still worried because ninety days was still a very fast sale for a home like theirs but they had a great agent who went above and beyond the call of duty and made it happen. As far as they were concerned, that agent was a super star, and they would always have the perfect answer if a friend in the area needed a real estate agent.

Tip: A great many home sales occur because of an employment opportunity that requires relocation. Here are some things to think about it if that is your situation.

1. Remember to manage expectations with your sale. That is especially important if your new home relies on the sale of the first.

2. An offer can be contingent on the sale of another property but that can be less attractive to a seller.

3. If an agent helps you in a relocation situation, you can show your appreciation with a referral or two, especially since you know they will take care of whomever you refer.

LOUIS AND ARABELLA MAKE THE DECISION

They deserved it. They needed it. There was no doubt about both of those things. Louis and Arabella had worked very hard and lived very frugally. They had not only paid their mortgage according to the terms but over the last seven years, they had also paid the principal down significantly. Their starter home was small and now they had two kids. So, they did not hesitate but made an offer on a larger home in a nicer neighborhood. The offer was accepted and they had no trouble obtaining financing. Now came the decision. Would they sell the starter home or would they keep it and rent it out? There were advantages to both possibilities. The issue that really decided it for them was location. They wanted to invest in property but they wanted property a little bit closer to them. So, they decided to sell but they committed themselves to taking the proceeds to find investment property close to them. They were happy they told the agent selling their home all about it because she not only helped them sell the starter home but came up with several possible properties closer to their new home. They were overjoyed. Everything had worked out absolutely perfectly for them and for their goals.

Tip: Sometimes, making a decision as important as selling a home can take a great deal of effort and thought. Take your time! Here are some thoughts.

1. Try your best to make the decision taking your emotions into account but not based solely on your feelings. It is critical to make decisions like this with a good deal of logic.

2. A good first step is to determine what the practical implications of a sale or of keeping a property might be. From there, the decision can be made with all of the facts in mind.

3. When you use the proceeds of one real estate sale to buy other real estate, there are often tax benefits. Speak with a professional for advice in this regard.

LUKE AND LACEY FOLLOW THE ADVICE

Luke and Lacey felt a bit lost. They were both very successful. In fact, Lacey was in senior management at a large financial firm. Luke's business now had seven locations. All of that, and they were only twenty-five! When they decided it was time to get a little bit larger home that would give more room for their kids and their dogs, they were raring to go. They met with an agent and hired her and a little later, Lacey and Luke had a heart to heart. Lacey shared that she thought maybe they came across as a bit arrogant. In fact, she was certain they had behaved with a great deal of arrogance and she was not happy about that at all. If they were going to succeed, they needed to be teachable no matter what accomplishments they had in their history. They humbly picked up the phone and put the agent on speaker phone. Luke explained that they were very successful and sometimes they let that go to their heads. Instead of just directing her, they really should have asked what advice the agent had for them. The agent told them the call was very appreciated and began to share some ideas. Almost immediately, Lacey and Luke realized just how valuable the agent was going to be. There were ideas they never would have considered and they appreciated the agent was still willing to share them.

Tip: A good real estate agent has a great deal of experience that can be applied to your situation. This is why you should carefully consider any suggestions he or she make.

1. Whatever situation arises during your sale is very like something your agent has previously dealt with or something another agent in the office understands.

2. Real estate is a specialized industry and relying on your agent's expertise is sometimes critical.

3. Being teachable and listening to your agent's advice does not mean your agent should not be accountable to you. The key is finding the balance.

MATTHEW AND ELEANOR GET IT DONE

Matthew and Eleanor thought they could do it. They had anticipated thirty days but there was really no reason they could not do two weeks. They were especially happy about the idea because the offer was a full five percent higher than the asking price just to vacate sooner. The only real sticking point was that their new home would not be ready. That would not really be a problem. They could stay with family for two weeks. However, they would need to figure out what to do with their stuff. Their agent suggested figuring out how much it would cost for the movers to store their things for two weeks. They could counteroffer with those charges added to cost. They decided to follow their agent's advice and they made the calls. The price was not even an extra thousand dollars and they were inclined not to require it but the agent explained the buyer could always come back with something else. They felt it would be better, since the buyer already offered a higher price, to just let the price stand as it was and let it go. Even if it was not the highest price they could get, they felt like it was the right thing to do. Ultimately, feeling good about doing the right thing was worth far more to them than anything else.

Tip: Sometimes, a buyer has a great deal of urgency and one of the important selling points for them will simply be a quick move. Here are some thoughts.

1. If you can manage to vacate your property early, that may help get a better price in some situations.

2. Remember to consider the impact on your life and the transition involved if you leave early. The buyer should compensate you for both your inconvenience and expense.

3. Remember to keep a win-win attitude in mind. Not only will you feel good about a win-win transaction but you will also reduce the chances of bad feelings or problems later.

NATHAN AND ANNIE MAKE THE SALE

Nathan and Annie were open to some version of the plan the buyer suggested but there were some terms they were not completely confident about. The biggest concern was that the buyer wanted to take possession of the house during the escrow. They understood that the buyer's sold home was due to close escrow in just a week but they worried that giving possession of the house over to them before the transaction was complete could be a real problem. The extra thousand dollars they had added to their offer did not seem to cover that risk. Their agent told them to think out of the box. He called the escrow company and got commitment to close within twenty days. Then, he suggested they reduce the cost of the home to their asking price and tell the buyer to use the extra money they offered to cover the cost of a hotel until the home closed. They did not know if the buyer would agree but they were pleasantly surprised when it happened. They were grateful to the agent for thinking about solutions and they were grateful for the buyer for seeking a situation where everyone won. As they moved on to their next big adventure in life, they decided they would take what they learned from the experience and put it to use in the rest of their lives.

Tip: Do not forget that it is the job of the real estate agent to negotiate on your behalf. Here are some ideas to keep in mind.

1. Your agent receives a commission and the payment is for every aspect of the sale. This is why making certain of the agent's qualifications is critical for you.

2. Your agent should help you find solutions to problems to progress toward a sale.

3. The best solutions do not have a loser but two winners. When you seek circumstances where all parties end up ahead, you end up with better outcomes.